G000114729

The Panacea Principles
By Allen Martin

Helping you discover the truth and wisdom in your life

ISBN: 9798740692487 KDP AMAZON

Foreword

Hello and welcome to The Panacea Principles.

I have the honour to share some simple reframes which have come from my many life experiences and accumulated wisdom. You will be able to use them immediately and I hope that they will have a huge impact on your life too.

In each chapter, I will explore many areas of psychology and apply easy to understand questions for you to ask yourself and suggest ways to shift your mindset.

The book will take you on a journey of personal discovery and self-development that will allow you to see the world through a different lens, and to help you to be an even better version of yourself.

At the end of each chapter, there is an **Inspirational Thought** to help you TAKE ACTION and REFRAME YOUR MINDSET.

I have created pages on social media called the Panacea Principles so that you can stay in touch and I would truly value any feedback, thoughts and ideas that you may have.

Welcome to the Panacea Principles.

"Panacea"

Panacea is a combination of two Greek words: 'pan' meaning 'all', and 'akos' meaning 'remedy'. It is derived from the Greek 'panakes', which means 'all-healing'. In Greek mythology, Panakeia was the goddess of universal healing; she was believed to have a potion that would cure any sickness or disease.

Chapters of Panacea

Chapter 1   –   Introduction

Chapter 2   –   Collect Moments Not Things

Chapter 3   –   The Frequency of Calm

Chapter 4   –   Finding a Happy Place

Chapter 5   –   Discovering Serendipity

Chapter 6   –   The Power of Music

Chapter 7   –   Animal Magic

Chapter 8   –   The Hundred Scale

Chapter 9   –   Empathic Listening

Chapter 10   –   Look for the Good Always

Chapter 11   –   The Power of The Pause

Chapter 12   –   Storytelling

Chapter 13   –   The Voices in Our Heads

Chapter 14   –   Reading Body Language

Chapter 15   –   Our 2 Monkey Brains

Chapter 16   –   I have a Dream

Chapter 17   –   A Sprinkle of Magic

Chapter 18   –   The Train of Life

Chapter 19   –   The Value of Time

Chapter 20   –   Covid 19

Chapter 21   –   Final Thoughts

Allen Martin –   Biography

Chapter 1
Introduction to the Panacea Principles

I wanted to start the journey, that you are about to embark on, with a story about a real journey of mine.

I was travelling on a packed London underground train a couple of years ago, and was lucky enough to have a seat in the rush hour. Lots of people got on at the last stop and standing right in front of me was a lady who I sensed might need a seat. 'Would you like my seat?' I asked. The lady emanated a sense of calm, despite being on a packed train at 6pm after a day's work.

She smiled and said, 'No thanks, I'm ok.' I said, 'Do you mind if I ask you something? What is the big dream in your life?'

She looked surprised by a total stranger's question, especially as we were surrounded by so many people. However, I had a deeper sense in that moment that it felt strangely safe and OK to ask. 'I have already fulfilled my dream,' she said. 'My daughter is at home when I get there, and she is all I need in the world to be calm and happy.'

As she said this, her eyes smiled with a deep warmth and pride. What she had spoken was her truth and we could both feel it. I got off after a few stops and she smiled at me, knowingly. It was a beautiful moment. She had told her truth in that moment – and to a total stranger. She was able to filter out the 'noise' on a busy train and access her deeper wisdom and truth.

At a deeper level, I sense that all of us are searching for calm in our lives and a sense of truth and purpose.

Our lives are so busy, there is so much noise and it feels as though there is nowhere to hide. It is the small things that are truly the big things, as you will discover as you read on.

The Panacea Principles is a story of many life experiences, learnings, places I have worked and people I have met that have led me to a place of calm and inner contentment. As you discover these stories and I share simple ideas with you that you can introduce into your life, very simply now, you will realise that peace, calm and contentment begin and end with 'self'.

You will only reach your own panacea if you complete the first step, which is knowing yourself more deeply. You need to love, understand and be proud of yourself, connecting with your inner truth and wisdom and in effect, your essence. You will need to create the inner belief that you deserve all the things that happen to you and that you are worthy.

If you are happy in your own skin and your own being, everything else will follow. The need for validation from a challenging world that barely has time to breathe and understand itself can be a thing of the past. Your happiness must come from within you and not from others who have a totally different view of the world.

You will notice that in effect we are all playing a different game on the same board of life – searching for our own truth.

You will see, feel, believe, and understand that the simplicity of loving and valuing yourself will lead you to be calm, content, in control and ooze an inner happiness that people will be able to sense and notice. This deeper connection and access to your wisdom will enable you to achieve your own personal greatness.

I have created the Panacea Principles in a simple to understand way with many ideas, strategies and simple reframes and interventions that you can use and take away NOW and implement in your life immediately. You can decide to use one idea or several ideas. They can be used independently or together and how you decide to use them in your life is totally up to you.

Thank you for joining this Panacea journey of discovery and I am looking forward to you experiencing many 'light bulb moments' as we explore the joys of being truly human and being true to ourselves and our beliefs.

I want you to imagine that you wake up tomorrow morning and a genie has waved a magic wand over your life. You get out of bed knowing that you have everything you need to accomplish what needs to be done in your day. This will not only make you happy, and you will also achieve everything you set out to do and more.

In this panacea place everything is possible. All avenues are open. No doors are closed. You are limitless and powerful, content and happy. You are so confident in this feeling that you bounce out of bed with a spring in your step, ready to face the world with a strength, power and determination only Samson/Popeye/Tony Robbins could dream of.

In a world that is busy with so much noise, our smart phones constantly pinging, thinking, and worrying about our family, our friends, how much money we have, what others think about us, we so often need consistent praise from others around us to validate who we are.

We think that when what we believe to be our true needs are met, that that will make us happy and calm our ego. How come for many of us this is not our truth. What really gets in the way of this happening?

Often our greatest perceived weaknesses are our greatest strengths. We are sometimes in fear of them, so we avoid them – yet they are the path to the panacea we seek. How do we shift our attitude and mindset to create a deeper belief and worthiness within ourselves that all is OK and to be aware that if all is not ok – that is ok too?

Life is so busy, and we often do not have time to think about these things. The Panacea will help you reframe areas of your life that you may experience as black and white. The Principles will give you some simple ideas to make your life vibrant with colour and opportunity again. That feeling of joy when you see a rainbow. It makes us feel like a child again – carefree and limitless. **That is the Panacea Principles.**

Over the following chapters, I will explore many ideas and ways you can reframe yourself and relax yourself to connect with your wisdom and your truth so you can feel calm within yourself at a level you never have before. Imagine this no longer, it can happen now – all you must do is follow some simple ideas.

You can also look forward to watching the videos and other social media that will accompany the book.

Welcome to your Panacea Principles journey.

Chapter 2
Collect Moments Not Things

I invite you to remember the memorable moments in your life. Those truly stand out moments that pop into your head immediately. Pause NOW and think of one or two.

They are going to be those truly significant moments that have lodged in your deep memory. They made you feel wonderful, they made you feel proud, they made you feel happy, they made you laugh, or they made you cry.

Your memory had an emotion or a sound or a smell or a feeling or a taste linked to it. It has created a deeper feeling that has stayed with you.

You are thinking of it now and the memory is flooding back. Where you were, what you were doing, who you were with and most importantly, **how it made you feel.**

The human mind is truly extraordinary. I would guess that you cannot remember a day last week when you went to work and nothing out of the ordinary happened, yet these long-term memory experiences on these special days stay with us.

They are the stories we will tell people when we meet them. They define us as humans at a deeper level, they expose our humanity. These memories mould us and shape us into the people we are today.

If it is a happy memory, your bodily chemicals will leap into play - oxytocin (trust and love chemical), dopamine (for the burst of joy), serotonin (creating a sense of wellbeing and safety). If the memory was something less happy - endorphins (which block perceptions of pain) and cortisol (which helps you relieve stress) come to help you.

This powerful cocktail of chemicals is there to help us through our lives and respond to both the happy times and the challenging times to create the feelings that those powerful and long-term memory events create.

Your happy memories are like diamonds. They are precious, rare and magical. Treasure them and value them. They are your deeper truth.

In the 21st century, society, social norms and social media have created a belief in the western world that the measure of anyone's success is what they own and not who they are. How happy, at a deeper level, do material possessions make us? You buy your new house or car or watch and then a week later it is the norm. You have got used to it and you are looking for the next thing. Do these things really give us what we need to be happy?

Conversely, you can be sitting in a modest abode, have the simple things in life and be totally content in yourself and in your own skin.

I had the honour to be in Sandton, Johannesburg, South Africa many years ago delivering a training course for HSBC Bank who I was working for then. After the training was finished, we visited Soweto – the township in Jo'burg. One of the employees of the Bank lived there and me and the Manager of the department visited her home. The home was incredibly modest to say the least and what I will always remember was the incredible pride with which the lady showed us her home. As we walked in, we were greeted with such smiles and love that the moment has stayed with me till this day. I sensed that she had found an inner contentment in her challenging world, valuing the things that really mattered to her - family, love and truth.

My belief is that the correlation between material possessions and happiness or longer term inner peace is a tenuous one. It is a myth perpetuated by the western world. As long as you have enough wealth to sustain yourself day to day with a roof over your head, food on the table and enough for a few small extras, any additional money for 'a bigger anything' is a nice to have only. It will sustain your contentment level for a short period but will not deeply affect your longer-term self-love and happiness levels.

As I said earlier, it has always amazed me that we seem to value people by measuring their success in terms of the material goods they have and not by who they are.

It is a powerful reframe. Who are you really?

Then something incredible happens when we pass away.

The moment someone passes away, there is a dramatic shift in the perception of that person. Out of the blue, we all start to think of the deceased person through a different lens. We begin to remember all the wonderful things they did with their family, how they helped make the world a better place with their charity work. In other words, we remember their 'WHY'.

In an instant, we reframed our belief and perception of that person. We rarely hear about the size of their material possessions as the measure of their success. This has always fascinated me, what is happening here? Why is this the case? What shifts in that moment of departure?

My sense is that it is the truth of that person's life that is revealed in that moment and the truth we all see is their 'why' and not their 'what'. Who they truly were.

Imagine a reframe now in your own life. You can alter the way you live, with a beautiful and simple change which will replace the way you act, believe, behave, treat and help others.

You can also start to think about what you want people to say about you and your life when you're gone. Start to live each day realising that every single person you meet will come away with a sense of you and a deeper belief about you. You will have 7-10 seconds to influence the new people you meet, since that is how long most people take to register their first impression.

Use every meeting or get together with anyone, whether you know them or not, to make sure you leave them with the impression that you are someone they like, someone they trust. You are building your own personal brand as you do so. You will be creating your own legacy every day of your life. What do you think other people really think about you? If it is not what you would like, you have the power to change it now.

I heard a wonderful story when I was at a funeral several years ago. The person taking the service pointed to the gravestone - it had the person's name and underneath, the dates they were born and passed away. In between the dates there was a small hyphen. The person officiating asked us what this hyphen represented. He explained that this small horizontal line represented the person's life. It was their story. That small hyphen will mean a totally different thing to each of you and will represent your unique version of that person's story. The hyphen was their 'why' and their purpose. How powerful is that message – and it has stayed with me forever.

Inspirational thought to leave you with.

In your life when you collect moments and not things it will immediately make your life fuller, richer, more meaningful and create the panacea for which we all search. These moments are your truth, these moments guide you, these moments are your essence, these moments are who you are and when you notice this, they will be your best friend now and forever.

Chapter 3
The Frequency of Calm

You may have heard of the 'Law of Attraction'. It is a now famous concept discussed in great length in the book 'The Secret' by Rhonda Byrne. We all emit a frequency, a vibration and an energy from our bodies. This is a powerful force over which we have no control and yet the power it emits is one of the most incredible and life changing forces we know.

This frequency reveals our truth to people at a subconscious level.

Others emitting the same frequency as you pick up on it. It is like tuning your radio and picking up the channels you enjoy listening to - we tune in to 'likeminded' people around us and conversely 'tune out' people who are on a different frequency – and therefore not like us.

Psychologists say that we become the amalgamation of the 5/6 people we spend most time with and connect with. Spending time with people who 'encourage you and make you feel good' will have a truly positive effect on your life.

It is an incredible, intangible and unexplainable thing when you meet someone who is vibrating on the same frequency as you. It just happens and it just IS. The room lights up with a translucent power woven into the fabric of the environment. It is magical and real and the invisible sparks fly. It is as if the 'truth' is revealed right before your eyes and yet you have no control over what is happening at all.

Conversely, spending time with people I call 'awfulisers' (those people who hang round the coffee machine at work complaining how bad everything is – and never doing anything about it). Spending time with these people will bring you down – you know who they are, as a name has just popped into your head!

When we release 'positive energies' into the world, we receive positive messages back. Conversely, when we send out negative energies, we receive these back too. It is all about our mindset.

Imagine that you can learn to emit positive frequencies more often. You will see and experience the world in a totally different way. Suddenly wonderful things start to happen to you. It is truly amazing and totally within your reach today.

Sharing a personal experience again, I was training a middle management banking group in communication skills at an offsite just outside of London, a few years ago. As they walked into the room and we shook hands, they were all suited and booted, all wearing ties and all 'well-groomed'. Having worked in the banking world for many years, this was no surprise to me.

I planned to open with a WOW! moment, knowing the audience and their general reluctance to come on courses, especially for a whole day.

I went over to the laptop and within 5 seconds James Brown – 'I Feel Good' was playing quietly in the background. I noticed some were responding to the music, so I turned it up louder, stopped speaking and started to 'dance' at the front of the class.

I asked, 'Who would like some exercise?' Half the class put up their hands and suddenly, to my complete surprise, 2/3 of the more senior people rose from their seats and started to dance and that 'gave permission' for the whole class to dance.

The feeling in the room was so incredibly lively - ties were loosened, jackets came off and as they all sat back down, the atmosphere was incredible, their mindsets felt calm, and it set the scene for a truly wonderful learning day.

Life is about creating an oasis of calm around you in this busy world with positive people and positive thoughts. Making time for reflection, time to connect, time for ourselves to be at one with ourselves and the world around us is essential for our wellbeing.

In this state of mind, we start to notice the others around us who are also in this place.

It is powerful, it is intangible and it is real. The people receiving and giving this signal have an aura around them of truth, of wisdom and a deeper connection that exudes an inner calm and understanding. It is beautiful. Truly.

Imagine moving your internal dial and tuning into people who have always been on that frequency but you were not hearing or listening to them because you were listening to a different channel. You will start to notice and connect with many people who are on this magical frequency.

It is a frequency of truth, a frequency of understanding, a frequency of wisdom, a frequency of learning, a frequency of love. It is a beautiful thing.

Inspirational thought to leave you with.

As you are reading this, what I am saying may resonate with you or not. It is OK which ever it is. I am hoping that in the future one of you, at least, will contact me to tell me you read my book and it's now your time too. We can then connect on the same frequency. It is a beautiful and special place and once you discover it – your life will change forever.

Chapter 4
Finding a Happy Place

A beautiful thing for all of us to do to create calm in our lives is to find a physical happy place where we can go to 'be at one with the world'. A place free from the hustle and bustle of our daily lives, a place to think, a place to contemplate and a place to 'JUST BE'. I think there is no greater gift we can give ourselves. Do you have one?

The happy place can act as a powerful anchor even when you are not in it. You can visualise it and recreate how you feel when you are in it. You can carry this place and feeling with you always. When you become aware that you are stressed, take a moment to reflect and experience the feeling of the panacea you have created with your special place.

I have found several happy places in my life and I cannot recommend them highly enough.

My main happy place is a bench in my local park in a walled garden which is truly beautiful. I walk into this magnificent walled garden and sit on a special bench that reminds me of my Father who passed away in 2002. He was a truly great and wise man and a mentor in my life in so many ways. I sit on the bench sometimes for hours after work, especially on those long summer nights. All the noise of the world flows away like small twigs flowing down a wondrous clear and silent stream.

I close my mind to the thoughts that pop in. If a thought does pop in, I make every effort to listen to it and then let it float away with the clouds in the sky above me or in the clear and wondrous stream I spoke of.

I am physically sitting on the bench and spiritually connecting to the beautiful world around me. The gentle tweeting of the birds, the clouds majestically rolling across the infinite skies, the trees gently swaying in the wind, the gentle and subtle breeze, the power, and majesty of the warm sun. Truly 'BEING' and 'linking to' the source of life is a magical thing. All your worries just float away. This is a panacea of happiness and contentment in a noisy and busy world. The small things are truly the big things.

When I have had some big challenges in my life, this was a haven of truth that I needed. It allowed me to recharge my energy to face the world with confidence, power, and strength.

I wonder if you have a happy place or places in your life? If you do, I would like you to imagine you are there, taking in all the magical sensations. Seeing what you are seeing, feeling what you are feeling, sensing what you are sensing, touching what you are touching and smelling what you are smelling. Take a moment to take it all in and notice what it does to your body and your mind. It is a panacea of happiness.

Another of my happy places is walking in the woods in my local park. I am lucky enough to have a magical park covering acres of woodland, lots of deer and many other animals. It contains miles of small lakes and streams. It is truly a magical and spiritual place. Sometimes I stop and listen to the silence. The sound of it is deafening in its beauty. I have found that in that silence my deeper truths are revealed and that it allows me to connect deeply within myself. It really does make all my troubles float away. It allows me to 'BE' in that moment – at one with the world and the powers around me.

One of my favourite songs is 'Let it Be' by the Beatles – a memorable and magical song which has so many powerful messages entwined in the lyrics. How prophetic are those words?

If you are Ok, just 'let it be' – be in the moment. The present is a gift so enjoy it and the future will take care of itself. I let all thoughts just drift away. Listening to the song for me creates a powerful emotional happy place anchor that takes me back to that moment and that 'state' when I listen to it.

Inspirational thought to leave you with.

Finding happy places in your life is so powerful for your own state of mind, wellbeing and mindset. Look for them, value them, cherish them and they will be places that you can visit again and again, and they will immediately shift your mindset into a place of serenity, calm and happiness.

Chapter 5
Discovering Serendipity

Serendipity - 'Seeing small miracles that are around you every day'.

Horace Walpole in 1754 – suggested by 'the three princes of serendip' – the title of a fairy tale in which the heroes are always making discoveries by accident and sagacity of things we are not in quest of '.

'You have not lived today until you have done something for someone who can never repay you.' - **John Bunyan**

One of the most beautiful and simple reframes that you can make in your life is to start to notice the millions of small miracles that happen around you every day. It totally transforms your life in so many ways, it is unbelievable. You will quickly notice that it is the small things in your life that are really the big things. Helping people around you in so many little ways and starting to notice and open your eyes to so many truly good things.

Serendipity is opening up a whole new AWARENESS filter that then becomes part of your life without any thought needed. It JUST IS.

Becoming aware of the miracle, beauty and magic of when you wake up every morning and you open your eyes and you can see, you take a deep breath and you can breathe well, you step out of bed and your legs are ok to support you, and you open the curtains, and you bathe in the beauty of our beautiful world.

You can see the majestic sky, you can see the dazzling clouds dancing across the sky and you can hear the delicate tweeting of the birds and the gentle wind rustling in the trees...that is serendipity.

Noticing the small miracles that are happening around us every day – not taking the things that happen to us for granted – as they are the important things, the truly important things.

We as humans are always looking for the big fireworks and the big events in our lives to give us meaning when it is all these small things that make life so powerful and beautiful.

From when my 3 sons were very small, I always said to them to do 3 good deeds every day – I had been taught this by my parents. They would come home from school and tell me the good deeds they had performed, from holding the door open for someone to picking up something that had been dropped or helping someone to cross the road. Now they are in their early twenties and these morals and values are still second nature to them. It is a beautiful thing to behold.

As you start a new day, imagine if you and everyone in your life had one overriding prevailing thought for the day. As well as making sure you are ok, how can you go the extra mile and help those around you bring a smile to their face, in even a small way?

Serendipity is the art of doing, seeing and being a part of small miracles that happen around you every day. Enjoy your day making small miracles for others around you – there is no greater gift to yourself and the world.

For many years, when I worked for HSBC - a big global investment bank, I had the honour of frequently teaching in Malaysia. Over the years I built up a wonderful relationship with many of the hundreds of staff in Kuala Lumpur.

One day I was teaching a Client Services course and I was feeling particularly unwell. I started the class, and I was sure I had a chest infection. I was struggling to speak and breathe, yet I was determined to carry on and finish the class.

I made it to lunchtime, and I really needed to get some help. Three of the class members said they would kindly take me to the local hospital to get some tests in the lunch break.

I said to the other students that I might be a bit late back from lunch as it depended how long I had to wait to be seen. The three kind students took me to the A & E at the nearest hospital about 20 minutes away by car.

The caring and patient nurses listened to my chest and before I knew it, I was being wheeled at speed to a heart unit where, within a minute, my chest was shaved, and I was wired up and underwent a heart scan ECG.

Can you imagine what was going through my mind so far from home? Yet, a strange sense of calm came over me – I knew I was in good hands.

Thankfully, my heart was clear. However, I did have a chronic chest infection for which they gave me antibiotics.

I will always remember the efficiency and the immense care and kindness of the staff in the hospital and the kindness of the people in my class for taking me to the hospital.

After 2 hours, remarkably, I was back in the class and I finished the session for the day. I am certain that I am one of the only people on earth to start teaching a class, get taken to hospital with a possible heart attack, and finish a class on the same day.

The whole event was utterly serendipitous. The number of small miracles that happened that day would stay with me for the rest of my life. Truly beautiful humans helped and guided me and took me to a place of comfort, safety and shelter and they looked after me like I was one of their own.

Inspirational thought to leave you with.

Serendipity is truly a beautiful thing. So many millions of little miracles happen around us every nano-second of every day. When we open our eyes to them and let them into our world, they transform our lives immediately from focusing on the noise and things we have labelled as challenging or bad and focusing on the good.

What serendipitous experiences do you think and believe have happened to you in your life? And are you now ready to open your eyes and senses to the millions of small miracles that happen around you every day – it will be the best decision you will ever make.

Chapter 6
The Power of Music

I have been listening to music for 98% of the time I've been writing this book. Music is life. Music is food for the soul. Music shifts your mindset. Music changes moods. Music is so immensely powerful for you in your life. It has allowed me to write with freedom and activates parts of the brain that make you happy, make you more creative and it brings back powerful memories.

As John Miles said in his famous song 'Music' in 1978 – '*Music was my first love and it will be my last, music of the future and music of the past*'. Listen to this song - it is so powerful.

Listening to music is a truly beautiful thing. It can shift your state in an instant. It magnifies everything around you. Whatever your mood, you can listen to a song that miraculously mirrors how you are feeling. You listen to the words and they somehow resonate with you at a deep level – now that is magic indeed.

If you think now of the most memorable times in your life, was music a part of those experiences?

Someone can put a song on and it immediately transports you back to a place from your past. Not only does it take you back to the place, it rekindles the emotions that were inside you at that time and makes them rush up to the surface like a tidal wave. It is truly transformational.

Why is music so powerful? What is happening within us when music is played?

Music is not only able to affect your mood - listening to particularly happy or sad music can even change the way we perceive the world, according to research.

Music and your mood are closely interrelated. Listening to a sad or happy song on the radio can make you feel instantly more sad or more happy and shift your state in a moment. However, such mood changes not only affect how you feel, they also change your perception. For example, people will recognise happy faces if they are feeling happy themselves.

Music has an even more dramatic effect on perception: even if there is nothing to see, people sometimes still see happy faces when they are listening to happy music and sad faces when they are listening to sad music.

I was recently running a course for a company and as part of the pre course work I asked the group the following:

Please think of a song that has a powerful memory for you in your life that now acts as a positive emotional trigger, taught you something unforgettable and that allows you to see the word even more clearly. (A photo may also be attached to the memory too....)

Please download the song onto your phone and we will share the experiences and learnings in the session.

The results were utterly breathtaking.

Many of the group had known each other for up to 10 years. When they played their songs, many cried. Many were transported back to the place and time of an event and the emotions shot to the surface.

Many of the group revealed things about themselves that others never knew and opened a whole new lens on their deeper desires, wishes, loves, thoughts, plans, hopes and dreams.

Some accompanied the music with pictures from the event itself which revealed yet another facet of their world.

It shifted the mindset of the whole group and created a deeper connection than any teacher could hope for – that is the power of music.

Music releases dopamine in our brains. Dopamine is our chemical that is a 'burst of joy' within us and the expectation of a reward. This reward can come in many forms from a physical manifestation, a spiritual connection, or a mindset shift. Something 'shifts' in our physiology that brings pleasure to us.

Brain imaging techniques in recent scientific tests reveal that dopamine release is greater for pleasurable versus neutral music, and that levels of release are correlated with the extent of emotional arousal and pleasurable ratings.

Dopamine is known to play a pivotal role in establishing and maintaining behaviour that is biologically necessary according to Dr. Robert Zatorre, neuroscientist at The Neuro.

'These findings provide neurochemical evidence that intense emotional responses to music involve ancient reward circuitry in the brain. To our knowledge, this is the first demonstration that an abstract reward such as music can lead to dopamine release. Abstract rewards are largely cognitive in nature, and this study paves the way for future work to examine non-tangible rewards that humans consider rewarding for complex reasons.

The study also showed that two different brain circuits are involved in anticipation and experience, respectively: one linking to cognitive and motor systems, and hence prediction; the other to the limbic system, and hence the emotional part of the brain.'

Inspirational thought to leave you with.

Music makes you laugh. Music makes you cry. Music touches your soul.

What is your favourite song ever? Play it now. Notice how it makes you feel and what happens to you.

Bring music even more into your life from today and immediately notice the change it makes to you and your mindset.

Chapter 7
Animal Magic

As a young boy I always remember my parents saying that they never wanted animals in our home, even though deep down I really wanted a pet. We had 2 lovely tortoises Becky and Sadie who we hibernated every year and they brought us so much joy.

It is incredible as we go through our lives remembering so many memories from our childhoods, so many happy and sad times and how they made us feel at a deeper level.

I had the most truly beautiful and happy childhood, and I always secretly wanted a pet, even though I never said it to anyone. It was never going to happen – so I left it. It was OK. It was how it was.

Fast forward to having been married for 20 years and 7 years ago, my lovely wife Claire started making noises at home that she wanted to get a dog. It is incredible how quickly, during the conversations about getting a dog, my immediate response was a curt NO.

I had been programmed this way all my life – this was the way it had to be. Humans are complicated creatures as we know. The more we use the neurons within our brain the more myelinated they become. *(Myelin is a sticky substance that attaches itself to the neurons to make superhighways of thought and behaviour in our brains.)*

It is like travelling down the path of least resistance. Akin to travelling down a motorway of thought as opposed to travelling down a dark road in the country at night without your lights on – you will choose the path of least resistance every time.

That is why it is so challenging to reprogramme behaviours within us, and the motivation and dedication needed for this to happen.

And then it happened. I came home from work on a Thursday, I distinctly remember the moment. I walked into the kitchen and in the extension was this huge cage, and in the cage was this gorgeous small fluffy white Cavachon (cross between a Bichon Frise and a King Charles Cavalier) called CHARLIE. I know you will not understand this – my feelings as a boy kicked in and even though deep down, I knew I would be ultimately happy, a part of me still did not want the dog in the house.

Friends with dogs came over and lauded how beautiful he was. Everyone was so happy in the house with this wonderful addition – except me.

I was not allowed to have a dog, was I?!

Still, I felt uncertain.

For the first couple of weeks, I still felt this way until one day after a few weeks, something clicked inside of me. I have no idea to this day what the trigger was. It was like my truth had been revealed and I had slowly been reprogrammed.

The dark road in the country at night without your lights had slowly become a highly lit motorway in the bright sun.

It was a revelation.

I had a new friend. Man's best friend indeed. It was a beautiful moment. Fast forward 7 years and we are inseparable. I have 3 human sons and 1 canine son now. He follows me everywhere and we are truly best friends.

Whether you have had a good day or a bad day he is there when you get home. He runs up to you and the love that he shows is immeasurable. We release so many happy chemicals in this moment, it is incredible.

I also get a sense that they can feel our vibrations and energy when we are happy or sad. I have noticed increased empathy and him coming to be with me when I am feeling a little low or unwell.

I came home from a business trip a few weeks ago for 4 days. He heard the car pull up outside and he was waiting at the front door when I walked in. He was doing cartwheels all over the place, yelping and then he jumped on top of me and started licking me - and he would not stop for about a minute. That is how dogs show their love, affection, and loyalty to you. Truly magical.

Humans have so much to learn from dogs and animals in general. They are highly intelligent creatures, and their sense of smell and hearing is astonishing. Most amazing of all is their utter loyalty and love.

Dogs pick up when you are happy and they look at you in a certain way when you are sad that exudes magical empathy. It truly must be seen to be believed. It is like an instant magic potion.

Inspirational thought to leave you with.

Dogs are truth, they allow you to reveal the truth about yourselves – as do all animals. They bring you infinite joy and sometimes sadness when they pass away. They allow us to be free and be true to our own truths and wisdom.

I cannot recommend you having a pet enough if your circumstances allow it. It will change your life forever and will be the best reframe of mindset you will ever have.

Chapter 8
The Hundred Scale

The Hundred Scale is such a beautiful and simple reframe and concept that you can use in your life now and forever. Think about all the different, important things you do every day.

Welcome to the 100 scale.

A score of 100 denotes things that are major life events and incredibly important and events rated 0-1 are things that we do day to day that can be considered less life-defining and even mundane.

Most of the things we do in our lives most days score 0-1.

Where are we going to go at the weekend, where are we eating, are we eating meat or fish or vegan, should we go to this place or that, should we see this friend or that friend? On a scale of 1-100, most of the things we do on most days score 0-1.

Then suddenly, something of the magnitude of 100 happens. We may experience a bereavement of someone close, we lose our job, we get divorced, someone has a serious injury... something of that nature.

We find that in an instant we drop everything that we thought was important and immediately divert all our resources to the 100 issue.

How is it possible to leave behind so readily things that a

moment ago we considered to be of enormous importance? All the things we thought were important, that are really 0-1, disappear into the background.

Think NOW about a time in your life when this has happened to you. I would like you to reflect on what happened. How did you feel in that moment that you discovered the 100 issue and how are you feeling now? You will notice how far you have come. It is the 100 moments that truly define us.

My first 100 event was when my late Father was diagnosed with Non-Hodgkin's Lymphoma in 2002. I distinctly remember the day I found out like it was yesterday. The brain, as I always say, creates powerful deep memories with emotions and feelings attached. It was August 1st. It was a warm sunny day and I was at work in the City. The phone rang. It was my sister. She did not usually call me during the day. I sensed something may be wrong. 'Are you sitting down?' came the question. I gulped. 'Dad is having a nosebleed and it is not stopping. I have to be honest; it does not sound good.'

In that moment, my whole life flashed in front of me. Nineteen years later and my Father is still so prevalent in my life. Time has not dimmed the love and connection. You can imagine how I felt on that day. Dad sadly had stage 4 Non-Hodgkin's Lymphoma. The signs had been there in the previous 6 months. We noticed them and sadly never knew what they were. Dad had chemotherapy and at 76 years old and with a stage 4 diagnosis, he did not have a great chance of survival. He passed away peacefully on December 21st, 2002 with all of the family around him. We sobbed uncontrollably for an hour. It was a life defining moment. My Mother said I grew up in that moment. A 100 moment indeed. Our family and friends were wonderful as was my employer HSBC at the time. I always remember the love and support.

When a 100 event happens, we learn so much. We suddenly have access to resources and powers of knowledge and wisdom to do things we never thought were possible – to allow us to help people in a way we have never done before. To plan, arrange, organise. We truly amaze ourselves.

What is it that triggers within us when a 100 event happens that allows us to do this? I wonder if these powers are accessible to us to achieve even more in our lives during the 0-1 times? Imagine that were possible and what effect that would have on our lives all the time.

We notice the people around us who come into our lives to help and support us during a 100 event. We always remember who they are. The family and friends that step up and are there. We also notice and remember conversely the people who we thought would be there and for whatever reason were absent.

These are powerful times for us and the memories are deep. The mind controls us and guides us in fascinating ways. The brain is programmed for survival akin to us living in a cave 4000 years ago and the bear is charging towards us. The 'fight' or 'flight' instinct kicks in and we must make a choice. It is how we are wired. These are crucial times in our lives.

It is the 100 events that define us as people and how we cope and grow.

Inspirational Thought to leave you with.

This powerful topic makes us realise that we should not sweat the small stuff. We need to enjoy the day-to-day parts of our lives that we take for granted.

In our busy world that is getting busier, we all need to worry less and enjoy more. We need to let the 'normal' things just be. If you can do this, you will notice how much more relaxed you are, how much happier you are and how much more content you are.

Chapter 9
Empathic Listening

---

*'There is a voice that doesn't use words - Listen' – **Rumi***

*'We dance for laughter, We dance for tears, We dance for madness, We dance for fears, We dance for hopes, We dance for screams, We are the dancers, We create the dreams.' - **Albert Einstein***

On a beautiful summer's morning at around 6am, I was woken by the gentle tweeting of a family of red-breasted robins who nested yearly in the same tree in my colour-laden garden. I rose slowly and opened the curtains to marvel at the incredible, piercing blue azure sky, the branches of the powerful silver birch swaying gently in a light summer breeze and the cirrus clouds drifting majestically high in the sky. All was calm in the world.

Everything seemed so uncomplicated, no filters, no noise, no voices, no interference and all was as pure as the world intended it.

My mind was still and free and able to take in all this incredible peaceful nature.

I could truly sense the wonder around me.

Imagine if we were able to recreate this feeling and this mindset every day?

Imagine if we could all be fully present in our every

communication, allowing our inner wisdom to flourish. To 'dance in the moment with somebody', revelling in both a conscious and subconscious ballet.

Now, can you remember a time when you've danced really closely with someone special in your life? Or a time when you've watched Strictly Come Dancing in the UK or Dancing with the Stars in the US and other similar shows around the world?

You will have noticed that the couples who link and bond the best are not always the greatest, the most co-ordinated or the fittest dancers – what they do possess in abundance are the hidden connections that allow their bodies to move as one. They have a sense of 'oneness', they glide effortlessly 'in flow' together and their bodies are 'listening to each other' at a deeper, truly empathic level which powerfully connects them.

Notice how they are literally 'dancing in the moment' together, listening to the needs of the other – changing and altering as their 'personal opus' progresses, with a sprinkling of gut feeling, instinct and joined wisdom – until the incredible conclusion when they throw themselves to the floor, smiling, proud, confident and totally as one.

They await the judges' comments. As important and knowledgeable as the judges are – do the marks really matter? The judges have an outsider view of the world, they are not in the empathic 'oneness' of the dance.

The dancers have already entered the arena, dealt with the challenges and 'scored with the rapport'. In their minds they are already celebrating the moment at a deep level long before the 'seven!' can be heard and the board is held in the air.

I have wondered all my life if communication between two people is really a dance?

As a child we start to learn the simplest steps of this dance. Life seems so uncomplicated, easy and our minds are carefree, quieter, and receptive. We begin to have conversations with our parents, family, and friends. We start to notice and sense that the words will get us so far and that maybe to get what we want and need from the conversation, we may need to introduce a few more complicated 'dance steps' and a little raw emotion into the proceedings, so we develop our skills a little more subtly.

Then, we notice how others react to a louder voice, a quieter voice, we look at their eyes, we feel that we may need to adopt a new strategy to get the result that we want.

This is an important part of a child's learning – concentrating on the words but noticing that the real magic is happening elsewhere – buried under the surface in the body language and the way we use our voices, our eyes, and our bodies as one. We learn a whole new skill set to go with our words.......and then we start to grow up. We are having the same conversations using similar words, yet the dance feels so different, we are falling over each other's feet, there is often 'duality' instead of 'oneness' and it is often as if we are all listening to a different tune.

Very often when we have conversations as adults, if we are

being really 'true to ourselves', we can often feel that if our empathic listening skills were being adjudicated by 'the judging panel' we would be lucky to score a 'five!'.

Do you remember the words of the wonderful late Eric Morecambe speaking to Andre Previn in the famous comedy sketch? Andre Previn was telling Eric that he was playing all the wrong notes and that he was out of tune on the piano. Eric replied:

'I'm playing all the right notes – not necessarily in the right order.' I wonder whether he was closer to reality than he realised - or maybe it had a deeper meaning after all?

How deeply as adults do we empathically listen to people?

How often are we playing the right notes in the right order with each other?

We all seem to have so much noise, so much interference, we are always so busy, we are always in a meeting, out of a meeting, worried about so many things in life – do we really have time any more to deeply listen to people? I do not mean 'hear' what they say – I mean deeply and empathically listen to the exclusion of everything else as if you were the only two people on earth. Listening as much to what is not being said as to the words being uttered.

Noticing those nuances in someone's body language, that flick of the eye, a change in tone, an altering of the pace, a variance in the rise and fall that we used to be so adept at reading.

Imagine yourself as a master potter. You are standing there in front of your wheel and the 'formless' clay is ready to be moulded. You take your time and craft the most beautiful and incredible pot which you will show to the world. You have created 'form' from the 'formless' and understandably the world concentrates on the pot.

Yet the true magic is in the clay that created the pot.

I'm curious if the 'words' of our communication are the pot and the 'tone' and 'body language' are the clay.

Sometimes we need to look under the surface for the real reason why the pot turned out so beautifully, acknowledge it and celebrate it.

We need to ask ourselves why as a human race we have allowed the contamination of noise into our busy lives to get in the way of our beautiful listening dance.

Let us remember the innate skills and wisdom we learned as children to connect at a deeper level when we are listening now.

**Two can really become one when we communicate. **

I have always been curious if we all long for the day when we will truly listen to understand and not to respond.

We all long for the day when we will deeply and empathically listen for not what is being said, but for what is NOT being said. (Remember the clay and the pot metaphor always).

We all long for the day when we can truly dance in the moment together as if we were the only two people in the world.

And remembering how we opened this story - what a beautiful world it will be for all of us when we can wake up to that summer's morning at 6.00am, to a gentle tweeting of a family of red-breasted robins and see an incredible piercing azure blue sky. We will be able sense the calmness, the branches of the powerful silver birch swaying gently in a light summer breeze, the cirrus clouds drifting majestically high in the sky and we can all lean down and we all put on our dancing shoes together.

Inspirational thought to leave you with.

When you truly empathically listen, it opens a whole new world of connection, love, wisdom and awareness. You are not just listening with your ears, you are listening with your whole body and soul. Once you have discovered this, it will change your life forever. Let me know how you get on – I would love to hear.

Chapter 10
Look for the Good Always

I was standing on a wet and windy train platform some months ago with the wind and the horizontal rain buffeting me sideways. The whole line was delayed and my train was late.

In every situation in our lives we have a choice (except in exceptional circumstances) as to how we react to any given situation. Over the past couple of years, I have learned an important lesson. It is the most simple and powerful of messages.

Look for the good in everyone and everything, because it does exist. Sometimes we need to look a little more deeply to find it.

Another related powerful reframe is 'Love Not Hate' anyone and anything around you. This is also a powerful conscious choice we can make and I will refer to this later in the chapter.

This wonderful reframe of 'look for the good' will change the way you see, feel and experience the world. It immediately shifts your mindset into a positive and happy place. The fog, mist and the noise of life disappears and you know that everything will be OK.

As I was seeking inspiration for this chapter, I received a message from a very close friend of mine which contained the term 'Panglossian'.

This rarely used word immediately resonated with me and triggered wonderful and powerful memories.

In school I had studied French Literature and one of the books I read was 'Candide' by Voltaire written in 1759.

I remember that the book challenged me with many deep, abstract concepts I had never come across before and the biggest learning for me from the whole book was the character, Pangloss.

Pangloss was a man who was optimistic in every single situation in his life despite incredibly challenging circumstances. Terrible things continued to happen to him, yet he was always optimistic. This was his conscious choice.

Despite any adversity you are experiencing, always be optimistic, always look for the good and you will find it in the unlikeliest of places. Even in extreme situations in your life, when you think that there is no light at the end of the tunnel, the 'optimistic muscle' still exists if you can access it, nurture it and encourage it.

The Law of Attraction is a truly powerful thing. If you look for the good, good things will come into your life. If you focus on the negative, less positive things will happen to you. Our thoughts become our outcomes.

I used to teach 'Cultural Awareness' and in one of the sessions I used the example of a child brought up in a household with parents, family and teachers as direct influences. Let's imagine that this child has been brought up to believe that 'blue people' (I use this example as to my knowledge no one has been defined as blue) are not very nice and that the child needs to avoid them.

The child grows up with this 'believed bias', until many years later he or she starts a new job and lo and behold, their direct colleague is a 'blue person'.

The child's instinct immediately kicks in and their self-talk is saying, 'What am I going to do, I have been brought up not to like blue people?' They try to validate their belief with every fibre of their being because the belief is so deep rooted. They find themselves actively looking for things not to like about the blue person.

To the person's amazement and bemusement, as hard as they try to dislike the 'blue person', as they have been wired to do from childhood, they notice that the blue person is really very nice – a truly wonderful human.

There is now an incongruence and dissonance between what the person is supposed to feel and believe from their 'believed bias' and how they really feel.

I am curious if at a conscious and subconscious level we are all looking for the good in each other and I wonder at a deeper level, whether all humans do this as a default setting.

We want to look for the good in people when we meet them and if a person does not betray our trust, we will generally give them the benefit of the doubt and at a deeper level they make us feel safe.

This is important as we have a choice to look for the good even though we may have been programmed to believe otherwise. This is vital for our future evolution and success as a species as we enter a time when computers, robots and artificial intelligence (AI) are dramatically increasing.

In my life I have met a small number of people in whom, for whatever reason, I have not seen as much good as I would have liked. I sensed that something was blocking their 'good' and I was always curious as to why this was the case.

Many psychologists, including Carl Jung, offer theories to explain human personality and motivation to understand the world with regard to human interaction.

When we meet anyone for the first time and become aware of characteristics, we notice at a subconscious level if any parts of their personality and truth resonate with ours.

What we are really doing, using the analogy of a mirror, is noticing parts of ourselves that are reflected within others. We only notice parts in others that are also aspects of ourselves, otherwise we would be unable to notice them – it seems simplistic yet powerful.

What if we meet someone and for whatever reason we do not like them or something about them irritates us – what is happening here?

Psychologists call this the 'shadow' part of ourselves.

There are 3 main elements of the 'shadow' within us.

1. We may be noticing traits and characteristics in others that we do not like in ourselves.

2. We may be noticing parts in others that we would like to have. For example, if you sense that someone is selfish, it may be that you have elements of selfishness within you, but there is also the possibility that you are not selfish enough and that you are too selfless. A part of you wants to be more selfish.

3. We may be noticing a part of ourselves in others that is being repressed in our subconscious mind. Our subconscious is identifying with that trait or characteristic, even though our conscious mind is not aware of it.

4. A fourth option is that there is no reason for the feeling - it is your truth, which is ok.

In conclusion of this deeper analysis of relationships, everything you notice in someone you meet is at some level within you, whether as a mirror or a shadow.

I imagine that this will make you think about all the people you have met in your life and wonder which part of you they are reflecting – I know I did when I thought about this.

It also allows us to look at the different qualities within ourselves more deeply and how we can use the wisdom and knowledge to make ourselves even more aware. You can do this too – it is a gift for all of us.

In the same way that you are now choosing to look for the good in others, you can also choose **to love not to hate** everyone that you meet. This is a fascinating reframe when you first choose to notice it and then choose to embrace it. I have chosen to do this for a long time now and it has had a dramatic effect in many areas of my life.

My son helps me with this too when we are together. If he notices that someone or something is irritating me, he says – 'Love not Hate Dad' and it immediately triggers me to shift my mindset or at least investigate why I'm reacting this way.

So, from now on - If you notice, sense or feel that someone is making you unhappy – STOP!

Ask Yourself – is this true? And repeat under your breath LOVE NOT HATE – LOVE NOT HATE.

It is so simple and it works! I have found that after a while, using both reframes, I am a lot calmer and have started to question a lot of previous, deeply embedded beliefs – and now you can too.

Loving or hating is a choice we make for ourselves from a lifetime of internal wiring and experiences. It is our deeper gut sense speaking to us and our 'tummy brain or our second brain' keeping us safe and away from harm. I will speak more about the 'tummy brain' later in the book.

Inspirational Thought to leave you with.

Looking for the good in others is a powerful and life-

changing mindset that will alter the way you see and experience the world forever. It will take some time for this way of thinking to become who you are because you will be fighting your powerful 'ego' which will be wanting to see, feel and experience the bad. Using the 'love not hate' reframe will be essential.

With your tenacity, resilience and sheer determination to succeed, this new way of thinking will be a life game-changer for you.

Chapter 11
The Power of The Pause

'Create the space to find your truth and pause.' - **Rachael O'Meara**

'The pause is as important as the note.' - **Truman Fisher**

I have long been curious why something so formless, something so silent and something so often seen as inconsequential, intrigues me so much.

Often without the knowledge of the participants, it guides conversations, it leads and paces and when used knowingly, consciously, or subconsciously, it can be a powerful tool in our personal communication toolbox.

I have always been intrigued by 'The power of the pause' in communications. It is so valuable when used in your everyday conversations, in coaching and training sessions and in every telephone interaction. It enables you to glean so much more from the spoken word, increasing your awareness and taking your conversations to a whole new level.

If we look at the well-known Albert Mehrabian Model of Communication, we see that the spoken word accounts for only 7% of any communication, tone is 38% and body language is 55%. And yet in most societies and cultures, the spoken word is 'king' and forms the basis of most of our decision-making.

We wonder why there is so much disagreement,

misunderstanding and conflict when, with a little more understanding and awareness of how we are communicating, we can achieve harmony, understanding and ultimately a win-win interdependent agreement.

Imagine what could happen if we all took much more notice and became much more aware of the 93%? Wow – what a difference that could make!

How much are we aware of the 'Meta Game'.

The 'Meta Game' is what is really going on beneath the surface of the words when people are speaking to each other. The 'Meta Game' is the elusive and often hidden 93%, a small part of which we will explore today.

I like to think of communication using the metaphor of a cake. The words are what you can hear on the surface, so on the cake this is the icing, the candles, the bows, and ribbons making up the 7%. It is not until you cut into the cake that you can really taste its essence.

You find out if it is a Victoria sponge or a chocolate cake or something even more mysterious and exciting. It is only when we deeply empathically listen to the words and how they are said that we become aware of the pausing, the pace, the stressing, the pitch, the speed, the rhythm, the rise and fall, the emphasis to understand what is really being communicated, that is the 38%.

How many times has someone said something to you and the words were exactly what you wanted to hear, yet something just did not feel right. Your gut instinct, your inner wisdom was telling you that there was a dissonance or an incongruence between the words you were hearing and what you truly believed they meant.

You ask someone a question and notice a slight hesitation, a pause prior to their reply which gives you the insight that maybe some internal dialogue is taking place prior to the reply. As you notice this, together with other variations of tone and body language, you can probe further. You might say, 'I noticed when you replied to me that there was something else you maybe you wanted to tell me?' An open question like this will invite the recipient to speak further.

Recently, I was having a third coaching session with a client. A deeper rapport had been established over the previous sessions and we were exploring a subject for which the coachee had to search more deeply within themselves. I asked the question and then…. silence……and silence…and I waited.

Fully 2 minutes later, having searched deep within themselves, the pearls of wisdom that emerged were truly incredible and led finally, after lots of further interaction, to the ultimate successful conclusion. Any interruption of the internal dialogue would have broken the internal flow and the magic would have been missed.

For me, those 2 minutes were incredible, watching the coachee access deeper within themselves. I noticed the powerful body language leakage that was telling me that the 'cogs were whirring'. Their eyes were flicking erratically, the fingers were tapping lightly on the chair arm and they were 'moving' in their seat – something was really happening deep down.

Now, I am not saying that you should wait for 2 minutes in any of your conversations with people. What I am saying is, that often the first reply that people give you may be the 'first layer of the onion'. There is often so much more that people have to say before the conversation reverts to you.

If you are feeling or noticing that someone needs and wants to say more - a simple 'and', 'and then', 'anything else' or a plain and simple 'pause' will give the recipient some more time and space to go deeper. They will value the communication so much more and the response will be more colourful, deeper, and powerful.

In my experience, it is with these sorts of open enquiring communications that the true motivations of either 'need', 'want', 'desire' or 'problem' (the 4 core human motivations to do anything) are more likely to be disclosed. Often our deeper and true motivations are hidden well below the surface.

The recipient will very much appreciate your approach, even though they may not tell you immediately. They will perceive that you are listening more deeply, that you are empathising and that you are care about what they are saying. You will probably be doing this with people you already value and with whom you have a great rapport.

The challenge is to make every effort to do this as much as you can with everybody you meet. This will develop you personally and help create a powerful personal brand for yourself which people will truly remember.

It takes courage and bravery to listen to the silence, accept the silence and celebrate the silence. It is in the 'power of the pause' that the magic often happens.

Pausing and reflection is at a real premium in our busy world and the more we become aware of this – the alchemy of the non-verbal 93% - we will all begin to truly win the game.

I will sometimes be in one of the many group training sessions I facilitate and ask a question…and will wait and wait for a response. Everyone looks around at everyone else, and they look at me and I am sure they think that I have lost the flow…. and then someone will fill the silence and everyone breathes a huge sigh of relief - normality has been restored.

If no one speaks, I will ask, 'How did that pause and silence feel for you?' The responses are usually fascinating and range from total awkwardness to feeling uncomfortable to the rarer person who revelled in it.

It is incredible how many people in today's world find silence and pausing so awkward that they have a deep desire to fill the space. Silence is another wonderful tool that you can use in your communications, encouraging others to speak.

When you encourage your coachee to speak, by keeping quiet yourself, both of you benefit.

You can ask the open questions and your coachee is able to share their experiences and perhaps more and deeper information than they expected. Most people enjoy talking about themselves, even more so when they feel they are being heard. Your coachee will appreciate your deep listening and you will glean valuable, perhaps vital, information. It's a win-win all round!

There is a cultural need in most societies to fill silence. In 'higher context' cultures (Asia, Southern Europe, Middle East) developing trust in relationships is even more vital for doing business. It is significant that those cultures are more comfortable with pauses and silence and even celebrate the peace and quiet.

In our busy world in more 'lower context' type cultures (UK, France, USA, Scandinavia, Germany), it's go go go. Everything is 100 miles an hour including how we speak, how we listen and how we communicate generally.

Many of the great public speakers use the 'power of the pause' to build excitement and anticipation. Many famous speakers in history including Winston Churchill, Steve Jobs, Martin Luther King, Barack Obama and Bill Clinton used the 'power of the pause' to incredible effect – to galvanise an audience, to build anticipation and excitement, to take the audience on a journey and to help lead the audience to their own personal promised land.

Many of the traditional reasons that pausing is so powerful also merit a mention. Pausing allows us to process information, buys us time, positively affects our breathing and stimulates attentiveness. It really is the secret ingredient. However, it is imperative that all the correct elements of the communication are added in the right proportions and consistency. Otherwise the cake will not rise and the results, as with our communication will be flat and uninspiring. With the right ingredients, the cake will rise like a dream and all will truly enjoy and revel in the experience of the full 55/38/7 of communication.

Inspirational thought to leave you with.

In the silence exists the truth. In the silence we are truly BEING.

Pausing demonstrates confidence, authority, courage and gravitas and elicits a much deeper empathic relationship with the person or people with whom you are communicating.

Become more comfortable with your own silence and the silence of others.

Recognise the value of your own personal awareness of the 'the power of the pause' and 'the meta game' because these are the missing ingredients that will propel all your communications from good to great.

Chapter 12
Storytelling

My story starts as far back as I can remember as a very happy and very shy little boy. I was always so excited when it was my bedtime, whereas most children avoided going to bed, it was always something I looked forward to. My darling late Father would tuck me in and it would be time for my magical bedtime story and song.

My Father only ever spoke to me in French so I was very lucky to be brought up bilingual. 'Au clair de la lune' - my Father would sing to me, the song about the 'light of the moon', which would always precede the story. I still know every word of this song today - it had a powerful bonding tune and story.

My Father would then ask me to pick a country from the huge map of the world on my bedroom wall and then he would take me on a wonderful journey to that country.

I remember many of the stories so vividly, as if they were told to me yesterday – those colours – those smells – those feelings. They were filled with empathy. They were filled with emotion. They were filled with love.

Yes, it was the powerful and vivid words he used but it was also so much more than that.

We went on nightly journeys together, we went on magic carpets, we met genies, we went to the pyramids, we smiled, we laughed, we explored and we bonded. And then he kissed me goodnight and I could not wait till the following night for my next adventure.

Without me even realising it, my Father was giving me my first 'storytelling lessons'.

Every story my Father told me had a simple structure, it had a beginning, a middle and a close. It would set the scene beautifully - every story would take me on an incredible journey, it would hook me in, it would build my excitement, it would paint a vivid picture, it would make me use my imagination, it would create a plethora of emotions, it would make me feel important and it would always leave me wanting more – a whole lot more!

And then as I grew up and became more aware, I realised that even the simplest fairy stories we learned as children contained all these wonderful learnings. 'Once upon a time, in a land far far away, lived a beautiful maiden in a castle deep in the woods. She had a secret flying carpet and would fly to places and rescue people in need ....and they all lived happily ever after.'

Simplicity. Painting pictures. Creating emotion. Structure. Taking us on a journey. A beginning, a middle and a close.... easy!

Why do you think you can remember the small details of a meal that you ate on your last summer holiday in a cherished location, when you cannot remember what you ate last week when you got home from work?

Why is it that you still remember the emotion and feelings of an evening out with your friends for a special occasion 2 years ago, when you cannot remember the details of a work meeting 2 weeks ago?

Powerful Stories create Powerful Memories in our minds.

They create empathy. They create deep feelings. They create emotion. Stories are our essence. Stories are who we are. Stories are a large part of our 'self'. Stories allow us to share personal experiences in a safe and non-confrontational way.

Stories are truly incredibly powerful and link and connect all of us in so many ways.

The more stories you can tell using your imagination, the greater will be the amazing effect on your life.

If you reflect now, you will notice that your closest friends are the people who share the best stories. Funny that. You can sit down with them for hours and tell story after story and it comes so naturally – it is a beautiful experience.

You are both 'in flow' – the time flies and you look at your watch and you wonder where the time has gone? You have been immersed in each other's lives. You have been truly as one. You have been 'dancing in the moment together'.

Telling stories releases some powerful chemicals in our brains that bond us and link us as one.

'Oxytocin- the trust chemical' is known to promote social

behaviour, bonding and the ability to form normal social attachments. Dopamine, serotonin and endorphins – the so-called 'happy chemicals' are released when we tell stories.

We can feel these 'bursts of happiness' when someone tells us a story we love and we are reminded of a happy memory. Like all 'happy chemical bursts' these last a short time and for many people are what they live for.

Telling stories about ourselves is a very powerful way of linking with others. As we listen to someone describing an event, we search for a similar experience from our own memories.

Why are we searching for our own experiences? What does this give to us as social animals?

It allows us to bond. It allows us to link, and it allows us to gain trust. It allows us to feel a part of something special.

Most people love speaking about themselves and telling their own stories. If you are a willing listener, with empathy, you will have a friend for life. Really you will!

You have heard the phrase 'sell the sizzle, not the sausage'. The sizzle is the story, the emotion, the feeling – the sausage is the facts and the numbers. Creating rapport and a connection with facts and numbers will get you only so far. Our brains are wired so that all our decisions are made in the limbic / reptilian parts of our brains. This is where our pictures, stories, emotions, feelings, decisions, gut instinct, intuition are based. Our Neo Cortex – our 'brain risk management system' is where our speech and facts and numbers are processed and located. Listening to someone spouting facts may get your attention for a short time. However, you will notice that you will quickly start to get bored and your mind will start to wander.

You must remember to sell the sizzle!

We all have a 'universal mind' that links us together with an invisible thread of shared experiences in a collective consciousness that spans the globe. The more we can free our 'personal minds / ego' to hear and access 'the universal mind', the clearer our ability to listen becomes, the clearer the stories we can tell and the stories we can receive.

Inspirational thought to leave with you.

Next time you meet someone, either for the first time or someone you know well, tell them a story. Paint a picture. Set the scene. Take them on a journey. Build empathy. Build excitement and notice the incredible effect it has on the other person and on your relationship. Notice the positive effect it has on your life NOW.

Chapter 13
The Voices in Our Heads

Have you ever wondered about the 'voice' in your head that is always there in the split second before you say or do anything? This voice is truly incredible. It seems to be all knowing and it seems to guide us and determine how we feel, how our day is going to be, our mood, our reactions to other people and the world around us.

It sometimes gives us a belief and a perception of 'positivity' and sometimes a belief and perception of 'negativity'.

This voice knows us better than we know ourselves. We see it sometimes as our 'best friend' and sometimes as our 'worst enemy'. In truth the voice is neither. It is our subconscious mind speaking to us, guiding us and helping us to be the best versions of ourselves that we can be.

Are these perceptions ever true? How did we let 'this voice' into our innermost lives and our innermost thoughts and feelings? How can we better control the voice? How can we make the voice our friend?

I am going to give my voice a name for the purposes of this article. I'm going to call my voice Bob **(please replace the Bobs in this chapter with the name you would like to give the Voice – it's personal to you).**

Hello Bob. How are you today?

There has been a vast amount of literature created to explain the Inner Voice.

Is Bob our inner wisdom?

Is Bob our ego?

Is Bob our subconscious mind?

Is Bob our gut instinct / intuition?

Is Bob our protector from harm?

Is Bob our 'inner critic'?

Is Bob our guiding light?

Whoever Bob is, he is here to stay in all our lives, and we need to learn to get used to him, treat him with reverence, love and respect.

How can we as a 'collective human race' make Bob happier and more carefree, make him smile and laugh, make him tell us happy and fun stories filled with colour and passion and hopes and dreams and sandy beaches and endless sunshine? - because deep down we know he is there for good in our lives and yet we don't always hear him.

Often the 'noise of the world' gets in the way and the messages that Bob tells us and that we interpret and hear are very different.

Much popular theory seems to indicate that Bob is our 'inner critic'. Eckhart Tolle - in the 'Power of Now' refers to Bob, when he is giving us negative thoughts, as a 'Pain Body' and to notice when Bob comes to us and puts apparent obstacles in our way and tells us stories that negatively affect our mindset, not allowing us to reach our 'inner wisdom'.

Eckhart Tolle encourages us to notice where Bob most often talks to us. Bob speaks to us in many, varied places. For me, it's in the shower and suddenly, Bob comes and talks to me and starts saying things to me, starts giving me doubts, starts making me worry about things, I can't do this, I can't do that, this person said something – what did they mean? Why? Why? Why?

I have successfully started to step away from Bob and challenge him. Who are you? Why are you saying these things? Are they true? This is not really who I am.

YOU have the power and you have the control to challenge your Bob. Take back control of your life and challenge him/her. It really is ok!

You will notice when you start to challenge Bob that he will start to go quieter and then you will notice him start to fade away until suddenly he disappears. He has tried to control you and you have fought back.

In that space and in that quiet you have found inner peace, true inner peace, sometimes described as 'flow' - a place where you are peacefully mindful, a place where the true magic of your life happens.

You can shift your mindset by challenging Bob and taking back control of your life.

When Bob is telling you a happy story, embrace him, listen to him, love him. Celebrate him. You have accessed your 'inner wisdom' which is your most resourceful state and the one that will guide you to all the wonderful things in your life.

Get used to listening to Bob's happier stories.

One of the best the ways to do this is in a quiet moment. Find a secluded space away from the world.

I have found a quiet space in a park very near where I live in a beautiful walled garden and I sit on my magically named 'happy bench' and I talk to Bob. I can speak 'out loud' if no-one is around or in my mind if there are any other people! Do you think that maybe that is a step too far?

'Good Morning Bob, what a beautiful day – how are you today?' and if you wait – he will reply to you almost instantly. It is as if he is there living permanently in your mind. You will be astonished that he will answer you.

He will say 'Good morning, I'm fine thank you. You ok?'

Try it now…speak to your voice……. it is important to give him or her a name as it makes it more real.

You will be astonished that the voice automatically answers you. It is your inner self, your inner spirit, your inner wisdom talking to you and it is the most incredible thing.

The voice is your friend. In fact, it is your best friend. It is your inner YOU, your TRUE SELF. You have connected. You are complete. You are whole. You are one.

Sometimes you can be in conversation with Bob and another voice appears out of nowhere wanting to join in the conversation.

Let us call her Sally.

'Hello Sally. How are you today?' (You can give Sally a name that resonates with you.)

I often wonder if Bob and Sally are a different part of our subconscious minds wanting to make themselves heard. They are both talking to us to help us and guide us through our lives – if only we listened to them more.

A lot of the work that I do as a coach is enabling people to get their own Bob and Sally to speak to each other. They are sometimes known as different 'parts' of us and they have had some truly incredible conversations in sessions I have run.

I'm sure that at some point you have said to yourself, 'a part of me thinks this and a part of me thinks that'. These different parts are your own personal Bob and Sally and we can get them to have a conversation. It is incredibly powerful and life changing for many when they do. We can also then ask the coachee to notice the conversation that Bob and Sally were having and notice what they noticed.

Thank you for sharing this journey with Bob, Sally and myself.

Bob and Sally are really our friends. Our true best friends. Our true inner wisdom. Our true selves.

When they tell us a story which we interpret as positive, let us all embrace them, cuddle them, laugh with them, celebrate with them.

When Bob and Sally tell us a story that we perceive as negative and put challenging thoughts in our minds and give us a negative mindset. Challenge them. Query them. Step away from them and you will quickly notice they will fade away and retreat to a place far away leaving you motivated, smiling and happy with a truly positive frame of mind. A mindful 'flow' resourceful state.

......then come and join me on my 'happy bench' and let us all celebrate with our own voices together.

They really are both TRULY beautiful people and the TRUTH in our lives!

Inspirational thought to leave you with.

As you have just read this paragraph your voice is speaking to you now. What is it saying to you in this exact moment? Whatever it is saying is your unbridled TRUTH.

The voices are your subconscious mind communicating with you and guiding you through the challenges in your life.

You may not always think they are helping you and you must realise they know you better than you know yourself – as

they are your deeper wisdom, essence and truth.

Chapter 14
Reading Body Language

'Body language is more fascinating to me than actual language.'
– **Michelle Yeoh**

'What I really like doing is storytelling, finding the body language that is necessary for the story. And when I'm doing it and it's working, I'm thrilled.' – **Patricia Birch**

I have always marvelled at the subtle nuances of body language that take place beneath the words that we speak.

In a world that seems to be taken over by the internet, sophisticated algorithms and Artificial Intelligence (AI), we are losing one of the prime differentiators that ensures our ultimate survival as a race because it gives us that key communication edge.

It is our HUMANITY. It is our EDGE.

What can we do as a collective to learn to love and hone this powerful lapsing skill again?

As social media tries to become more 'emotional', evolving more ways to replace this once indomitable bastion of humankind.

How can we as a human race ensure that the beauty of non-verbal communication continues?

We know the real magic of conversations takes place beneath the wondrous words that emanate from our mouths. It lives in the subtlety of our tone, the deft nuances of our pace, our simple and powerful breathing, the rise and fall of our voices and our calculated and clever pausing – to name just a few of our core innate human interaction skills.

I came home from work a few months ago and my twin sons were sitting on the couch with 3 of their friends, all glued to their phones. 'I will be so happy if you would talk to each other,' I exclaimed. 'We are' came the cry – 'we are having a conversation on a chat group with 30 of our friends....listen,' and the perpetual 'bings' of the chatter emanated loudly from all their phones.

'We really don't need to speak to each other anymore,' one of the friends said.

I took a deep breath and headed to the garden to mull over this incredible phenomenon. Can this really be true?

Are we now growing up with a new millennial / Generation Z who no longer need to communicate in the way we have always known? What are the longer-term implications for our society as a whole? Do we have a collective responsibility to make sure that this subtle magic that really IS the communication does not disappear?

We can all make this happen now.

As we know 'people buy from people' and 'people buy emotionally and justify logically'. We are wired this way from birth. It is our key survival instinct – it is what makes us human. We are emotional creatures.

The beauty that is inherent in the words and beneath the words is too precious to lose and when one perfects these gems – it is like uncovering the 'holy grail' of experiences. It is this 'Meta Game', as I call it, where our true wisdom lies. It is the link to the subconscious experiences that make up our core selves.

The 'Meta Game' is truly priceless, magical and beautiful. It is the myriad, nay plethora, of subconscious and unconscious 'tells' and 'movements' that tell others what we are really feeling and thinking. The 'Meta Game' is where the truth of our communication lies.

Our subconscious mind is 30,000 times more powerful than our conscious mind. It guides and directs us in ways of which we are often blissfully unaware. Our subconscious mind can be likened to 'the Conductor' and the conscious mind 'the Orchestra' – playing the tune that it is told to play.

We all 'leak' and 'project' parts of our subconscious mind without our conscious mind ever being aware of it. It is happening to all of us every nanosecond of every day. It is happening to you NOW.

It is evident in the subtle tapping of the fingers, the slight shaking of the leg, the subtle flicks of the eyes, the slight shift in the chair. These are the clues to the 'Meta game' that indicate that 'noise' is happening in the subconscious and revealing itself in conscious actions.

Uncovering and exploring this new world enriches our storytelling to 'hero' levels. It allows us to join others on their emotional journeys and their deeper metaphorical journeys through life so that we understand their view of the world and we can empathically dance together.

You notice and open a whole new world that you never knew existed. Your communications become so much richer and deeper. You start to notice subtle tone and pace changes in people's voices that can lead you to the promised land of empathy and rapport building.

Your communications, whether with family or friends or in business closing a deal, will be immeasurably better.

Inspirational thought to leave you with.

Notice the next time you are speaking to someone. Give them your undivided attention. Look them straight in the eye. Notice the nuances of their words and body language, their tone, their pace, their breathing, their pausing and you will uncover a world of subconscious riches that will enhance your life forevermore and will make you ultimately even more successful in every area of your life.

Chapter 15
Our 2 Monkey Brains

What is really jumping about in our brains when we need to make important decisions affecting the rest of our lives? We feel the chemicals brewing, we feel excited and nervous when this inner magical mix of both opportunity and threat gets to work inside us.

'Do I want this, Don't I want this', 'Should I stay or should I go', 'Shall I take this new job or not' - we are constantly making emotional decisions about something and research suggests we make up to 70,000 decisions every single day – that is 48 every minute!

Now you can understand why this can prove so challenging and we seem on many occasions to be so uncertain. Up to 70,000 emotional decisions a day! No wonder we need some help and advice, so that we seek others' opinions. No wonder we can find it all challenging and we so often question our decisions even once they are made.

We need to understand that we make every decision emotionally and we justify it logically afterwards. There are very few if no exceptions that exist at all.

We are indeed emotional creatures. As already discussed, we have a plethora nay myriad of fascinating chemicals released by our brains – dopamine is for bursts of joy, serotonin for safety, cortisol when we are under stress, endorphins blocking our pain and oxytocin as a bonding chemical. Wow! what a mixture!

Our emotional inner decision maker is our well-known limbic/reptilian brain – also known in many areas as our inner monkey or chimp. It contains all our emotions, our feelings, our values, our beliefs, our gut instinct, our intuition and so much more – it allows us to survive, it is who we are as humans. It is our truth.

Our monkey is truly powerful and research suggests it is 5 times more powerful than our neo cortex – the rational / risk management system area of our brain that is our logical friend and where all our spoken language emanates from.

So how can we better understand the needs of our inner monkey and use them to access our truth to help us make the right decisions more often?

We all have so much 'noise' going on in our lives that it makes our 'monkey' nervous and restless. We often make key decisions when under stress and our cortisol levels are high which really effects our ability to make the right decision and access our true wisdom within.

We need to work hard to keep our monkey calm and peaceful. It is truly imperative for us to function at our best. We need to nurture, love and care for him. We need to take time to understand him better – what he wants and needs.

We need to surround him with likeminded friends who nurture and support him as well as challenge him. We need to free him from any cage of uncertainty.

4,000 years ago, when we all lived in caves, it was a lot simpler for the monkey. You were in the cave with your family having dinner after a hard day hunting and gathering and the big bear was coming towards you. It was a simple decision of 'fight or flight'. There was much less additional 'noise'. You made your emotional decision with a lot more ease than we do today. Life was less busy. It was often the only correct decision that allowed us to survive another day.

The speed of our lives, the pressures we are all putting on ourselves together with the new digital world are impeding our access to our inner truth and deeper wisdom. In effect, the 'noise' is limiting our access to the toolbox of tools that allows us to survive and thrive. We need to truly understand this as it is crucial for our personal wellbeing and survival as individuals and as a race.

We must all set our monkeys free again to make our emotional decisions with a clear mind.

When that happens we will be truly winning. We will make even better decisions and be truly free.

As well as our limbic / reptilian monkey brain, another less known friend also helps us to define our moods, stress levels and helps us in the most important of ways – our gut instinct or our 'Tummy Brain'.

As you read this you will know that at a deeper level this is our truth. So many of the key decisions we make in our lives are from 'our gut feel'. In fact, think of any decision that you have made which is not. So, what is the mystery of this additional 'brain' all we have within us?

In our stomachs we have a network of neurons that line our stomach and gut. There are surprisingly over 100 million of these cells, more than in our spinal cord.

This is not a thinking brain—it does not reason, write poetry or solve complex puzzles. However, mounting evidence suggests that our gut's health strongly influences our mood. All those neurons lining our digestive system allow it to keep in close contact with the brain, which often influences our emotional state.

For instance, when we experience 'butterflies in the stomach', this is the brain in the stomach talking to the brain in our head. As we get nervous or fearful, blood gets diverted from our gut to our muscles. We think that the brain rules our decision-making process but it is clear that our guts have a very profound effect on how we behave – that is the power and the derivation of the 'gut feeling' we all so often have.

Inspirational thought to leave you with.

Your monkey brain is truly your best friend indeed. Be aware of it, listen to it, value it – because more often than not it is our deeper truth and guides us to making the 'right decisions' about our lives, other people and challenging situations that we face. What is it saying to you right now, having read this chapter?

Chapter 16
I have a Dream

We live life from day to day, dealing with the ups and downs of this wonderful world of ours. I wonder if deep down we all have a dream that we want to fulfil which is our deeper purpose – if only we knew what it was.

My story starts in a healthy eatery in Whitechapel, London where I was meeting an ex-work colleague for lunch to catch up and discuss a few ideas.

After my colleague had left, I started speaking to a truly inspirational young man who was working in the eatery before going to university. We will call him Simon.

Similar to my earlier story of the lady on the train – you remember! - I asked Simon what the big dream in his life was. He replied that unlike Martin Luther King he did not have a dream – a great response that immediately got my attention.

Simon then added, "I am studying criminology at University with the opportunity of an extra year's masters." After a long pause for reflection, he said that his big dream was to work in forensics and help solve crime to make the world safer.

Wow! I thought, what a truly incredible dream, especially as only a few minutes ago, Simon had been certain that he had no dream at all.

I wonder if we all have a dream within us that for some reason we don't even want to think about or acknowledge. It might not come to the surface as quickly as Simon's, though I'm certain it is lurking in all of us somewhere. Sometimes we just need someone to ask us the right question.

The rise of the internet and social media is reframing how we see the world and the dreams we have for ourselves.

I'm sensing that our purpose and dreams are being replaced by our need for 'likes' and validation from others. When we really analyse them, we realise that they don't give us the deeper satisfaction that we crave.

With social media, we are now becoming our own personal idols. This inevitably distracts us from achieving our greater goals and dreams.

As discussed in the previous chapter, life is made up of small moments that determine our dreams and outcomes. Technology is now so prevalent and supposedly connecting us, but I sense that many people are still feeling alone.

In the western world our dreams seem to be mainly material - bigger house, bigger car, more holidays.

I am curious to know if our dreams are really more personal and more cathartic. Perhaps more about learning and developing ourselves in order to find a place of contentment and fulfilment, through helping others and ultimately making the world a better place.

I am also curious to know if the dream is to get to know our 'self' better, to feel comfortable in our own space and with our own thoughts. And to feel comfortable with the silence we experience when we are alone. These silences, pauses and times of reflection hold our deeper truths.

Imagine being in a place where you are truly comfortable in your own skin and JUST BEING. JUST BEING in the moment, accepting the moment as it is and not having to ask any questions. Imagine.

This sounds like a real cliché, yet it is the truth for so many of us.

We work all our lives to provide for our families. Life is often not easy for many and we must fight to survive and thrive.

Having a dream ignites us and gives us a deeper purpose – a dream is a magical spell that inspires us into action.

Inspirational thought to leave you with.

Take a moment now to think about yourself and your life. What is the dream that you have for yourself in your life. What does it look like, what does it feel like and sound like?

Close your eyes now and take a moment to notice the first thing that pops into your head. It is probably your truth and once you acknowledge it, then you can chase it – it will change your life forever.

Chapter 17
A Sprinkle of Magic

We all have something in our lives, that sprinkle of magic, that is the source of untold wisdom, yet we are not aware of its existence.

There has been something in the way, a mist, a fog, a haze.... some noise, or maybe you were not ready. It was not your time.

It is hovering there like a quiet wizard, always in sight, yet totally inaccessible. Even though we can see it, feel it, touch it, we have never dared to reach within.

When you discover it and the small flicker that has shone quietly all your life turns into a huge flame, it is truly one of the most powerful moments of your life.

It opens doors that you did not know were there, it allows you to enter rooms and see and sense things of which you were totally unaware before. It creates a spark within that lights up your life like a volcano.

It is there within all of us and I would love you to share your experiences of when this has happened to you.

When you reconnect with this **source of life** everything immediately becomes calm and you know that everything will be ok.

Being happy in your own skin about who you are, how you act, how you behave towards others and the belief you have in yourself, leads to a deeper calm that will propel you to achieve everything you ever dreamed of.

Seeking validation from any other human as a key barometer of your own personal journey will never satisfy you at any level nor give you what you are looking for.

You may connect with the source through meditation, religion or personal truth, and once this happens to you, the small flame that you sensed had been burning all your life will ignite and burn bright in your life.

You can see it and sense it in someone's face. It comes alive. It is smiling. It is fully aware and deeply content.

One morning recently on the radio, the famous ex Arsenal footballer, Ian Wright, had everyone listening in tears when he told a truly magical story.

Recording a programme in a football ground, Ian was surprised when a man came towards him. Ian recognised him after a moment and immediately burst into tears.

It was a sob from his soul.

The man was his schoolteacher Syd Pigden, who taught Ian when he was 7. He told Ian that he believed in him and that he could achieve anything he set his mind to. Everyone else in Ian's life always doubted his abilities.

The deeper memory of Syd Pigden's words had stayed with Ian and in a flash the memory flooded back.

It is incredible how quickly a memory with an emotion attached comes to the surface.

The teacher told Ian that even though he fought as a pilot in World War 2, his greatest ever life joy and proudest moment of his life was seeing Ian play for England.

Ian kept crying and apologising and told Syd he was the greatest influence on his whole life.

He did not need to worry - we were all crying with him.

One of the greatest moments of radio I have ever heard.

This interview connected Ian Wright to the source of life itself, this deeper feeling within him that connected him to his truth, and it gushed up to the surface like a volcano engulfing him.

These moments are what we are truly about. Embrace them and cherish them when they happen to you.

Inspirational thought to leave you with.

Having read this wonderful story, I am curious what the 'Sprinkle of magic' is in your life that has just popped into your mind.

Chapter 18
The Train of Life

I wonder if we can equate our lives to taking a train journey. If you imagine the train journeys you have taken in your life, they were always taking you somewhere memorable, whether to work (yes this is memorable too in some way!) or on the holiday of your dreams.

There has always been something fascinating for me about taking a train. It takes me back to going to the seaside with my parents when I was a boy and we took the train round the pier and along the promenade.

I remember so distinctly that some people used to take the whole journey and some used to get on halfway through and get off after one stop and I always asked my parents why people did not stay for the whole journey – it was so much fun. It only struck me later how significant this was. Even writing this evokes so many memories and takes me back to those happy times.

It made me think that our lives echo this simple journey. Some people in our lives come along for the whole journey of our life (our parents, some siblings and other family and friends), some for a few stops and some for one stop only.

We meet all these people for a reason in that moment irrespective of how long they stay in our lives and on our journey. We have something to learn from each of them and they learn something from us.

If I reflect on my life, as you are now with your own personal train journey, it is incredibly powerful. I remember some people who I now realise that I met for one stop only but who truly came along at the right time in my life. They guided me, helped me and gave me critical advice when I needed it, then they faded into the background, although always there, but absent from the main part of my life.

I remember friends that came and went through my life at different times, both as a child and as an adult, and those I have fleetingly reconnected with over the years at weddings, funerals, birthdays and other functions.

My best friend at school was a boy called John and we were inseparable. We lost touch for over 30 years and incredibly last summer, I was sitting with my family having lunch outside in a local park when I heard my name being shouted. "Allen Is that you? - it's John from school." It is amazing how the instant memories of being back in school flooded back. After we introduced each other to our families, we proceeded to spend a full hour speaking about schooldays, who we are still friendly with and so much more. John had been on my train early in my life and the feeling was still there – those deep childhood friendships never go.

My teachers at school had a huge influence on my life. My history teacher Doctor Wheaton (going back 38 years) taught me history in one of the overflow classrooms. Learning about Italian Unification in 1871 with so much zeal and enthusiasm, I remember the minutiae of it to this day.

We never really know how long anyone will stay, apart from

our core family and friends, until we look back and reflect on our lives.

If we knew what the outcome would be, it would alter the way we act, behave and 'BE' in the relationship with that person, and that would change the magic and truth of all our relationships. It is not knowing that is the beautiful part, enjoying the 'ride' and the sharing of wisdom and experiences as they happen.

This is truly the great beauty and curiosity of our lives. It is only when we look back that we know how long each person stayed and perhaps the purpose of us meeting.

I have found it therapeutic to look at all the relationships in my life in this way with the metaphor of a train. I hope that you are enjoying your journey and whoever is on your train with you.

Inspirational thought to leave you with.

Reflect now on your life and your own personal train. Who has been on your train your whole life, who has been on for a few stops and who has been on for one stop only? It is a truly beautiful thing to do. It will surprise you.

Chapter 19
The Value of Time

Time is a constant in our lives every moment of every day, something that permeates our truth and is one of the most valuable commodities we have.

We often take it for granted, we do not use it as wisely as we should and we often abuse its majesty and privilege. Time is truly one of the most valuable assets in our lives, when we take the time to notice it, cherish it and become even more aware of it.

I remember so powerfully when I was growing up in London as a young boy, there was a square green playing space at the bottom of my road and in the middle was a sundial. I was always fascinated with time and how the shadows of the sun could be so pinpoint accurate, letting us know when we had to go back home after playing outside all day. Sundials originated in Ancient Egypt and Ancient Greece and calculate time as the sun moves from east to west. It is still a powerful memory for me today and links me with happy times.

Time is the one thing in our lives, no matter whether you are a billionaire or a pauper, that you cannot turn back or change – and yet it is as valuable to us as the air that we breathe.

I like to think of time as being an 'illusion'. What do I mean by this?

You can be doing something that you love and the time flies in a way that does not seem possible – you wonder where it went. Think of a time in your own life like this now! You can start the evening with wonderful friends talking away, laughing, smiling and joking at 20.00pm and the next time you look at your watch it's 23.00pm – where did that time go? it didn't seem possible and yet it was.

And then on the other side of Time - you can be doing something that you do not enjoy and every minute seems like an hour – you can be sitting there watching the seconds go by and the seconds last an eternity.

You are now thinking of your own life and when this happens to you!

How is it possible that the same 'time' can give us such different experiences, create such differing perceptions and perspectives, be such an emotional rollercoaster and make us feel so different within ourselves?

That is the power that Time has over us – and most of the time we are utterly oblivious to it.

We must realise that man has created time. Time is not real. Time is not true. Time is a construct only. Time is purely how we see it, feel it, sense it and experience it. Time is man's invention for an orderly way for us to live our lives and create order within a global system.

When we take a moment to think about it, it is one of our most precious commodities, yet it has illusory qualities that are verging on mystical.

We cannot touch time, feel time, taste time, hear time – yet it surrounds us every moment of our lives. Time leads us and guides us and we all have a certain amount of time on this magical world of ours. We wake up every day and we have 86,400 seconds in every day.

Wow! This is so many – how much true use do we make of this asset?

It is more precious than diamonds and it deserves so much more of our attention, respect, and love. We really take many things for granted and time is one of them.

Imagine after reading this that you start to notice time more and you start to plan your life to use it more wisely. You can learn new skills, you can read, you can travel to places you have always dreamed of.

If you now think of your greatest life memories - they will be a holiday, when you got married or had children, they will be the places you visited, the feelings at the time that lodged in the deep memory part of your brain and now stay a lifetime. These are the times you remember, you value and will be your most precious.

Time is also valued totally differently in different cultures in the world. Time is more relaxed and fluid in high context cultures. By high context I mean those cultures that communicate in ways that are implicit and rely heavily on context, emotion, body language and trust. Examples of high context cultures include Japan, most other Asian countries, most Arab countries, Latin America, most African countries and Southern Italy, Southern Spain and Southern France.

Time is fluid in these cultures. It really does not matter much if you are on time for a meeting or take longer for lunch. These cultures spend more time enjoying and celebrating life and being with those they love and their families.

In contrast, low context cultures are those that communicate information in direct, explicit and precise ways. Building relationships is important, however, less important than making decisions and getting the job done what are paramount. Examples of low context cultures include -

Germany, Norway, Denmark, Sweden, Finland, Canada, UK and the United States.

Why is knowing this important? It is hugely valuable in both the business world and your personal life knowing how different cultures value and treat time. When large companies have offices in different high and low context countries, it is invaluable to know how to act and behave when the different culture contexts mix and work with each other.

I adore using my time to walk in the woods near my home with my dog Charlie. I love my time spent with him and the magical use of this time will be something I will always remember and cherish fondly. It gives me time to be alone and time to think away from the noise of the world. We all need to recharge our batteries with quiet reflection to power ourselves up for the challenges of our days.

I also adore walks on the beach by the seaside and make every effort to do this as often as I can. On recent holidays in Spain, I used to get up early every day while the family were still asleep and the world was quiet and walk along the beach for a couple of hours, taking my time to notice all the beautiful things around me. The sea, the waves, the gentle breeze, the feeling of sand between my toes and picking up stones and shells which are in front of me now around my keyboard as I am writing. They bring back beautiful and powerful memories of how I chose to use my time so wisely for my own gratification. You can do it too – it really is ok. You are allowed you know.

A few years ago, I was working for a company which insisted that everything and everyone had to be on time all the time otherwise the repercussions were severe. Anyone late for a meeting would feel the wrath of the people who valued punctuality too much. This can be labelled both good and bad as all meetings were on time, yet some of the emotion and spontaneity were missing.

There is a famous story of a new CEO at an American Investment Bank. It was 8.00am on a Monday morning and he summoned all his new Executives to attend the first breakfast meeting. The Chief's secretary stood by the door as the time counted down to exactly 8.00am. 7 of the Executives had arrived and 3 were yet to arrive. The door was closed at 8.00am on the dot. The other 3 turned up at 8.01am as the lifts had held them up. They attempted to open the door to the meeting but the glass door was locked. They were advised by the secretary to remain outside the door for an hour while the meeting took place and at 9.00am the new Chief came out and told the 3 executives that they would never be late for a meeting with him again – they never were!

Time is a fascinating and fickle mistress - it can be used in so many ways – to create emotion, to provide order, to exert power, to create priceless lifetime memories and to gain control.

As a valuable addition to your life now, learn to notice time, learn to value time, learn to notice that it is our most precious commodity. Smile at it. Appreciate it. Celebrate it. Value it and use it to your advantage.

Inspirational thought to leave you with.

Control your time and do not let it control you.

Spend more time in your happy places, spend more time with people that you really like, trust and value, and spend more time with people who make you smile and be happy. Life is precious and short – use your time wisely.

Chapter 20
Covid 19

In early 2020 something happened to the planet of gargantuan proportions that when history looks back and judges, will have changed the world forever.

As I sit here in early 2021, we are all still in lockdown during the Corona Virus emergency. Never has the famous saying '**It is what it is**' become so powerful and poignant.

We seem to have entered a parallel world where we are now being asked to stay home 'locked down' for an indefinite period that may be as much as 9 months and possibly even longer.

It has been fascinating to notice the behaviour of the people around me. Some people are seeing Covid as a 'removing of liberties' and 'being in isolation' and others are seeing it, including myself, as a truly wonderful opportunity for self and personal development and a period of wonderful reflection and time with the family.

What I find truly remarkable is that as a human race over many years and generations we have built up patterns of behaviour along myelinated neurons in our brains of how to act, how to behave and how to believe - and a virus, a millionth of a millimetre in diameter has reprogrammed the whole human race in an instant – and the human race has not resisted and in fact has embraced the changes in the most remarkable way.

'Social distancing' and 'self-isolation' – terms that go against every human inclination for connection and joint dependency, have become the norm so quickly – and the population has been 'begging' the government to employ even more draconian measures to keep the population home and the population isolated. A truly remarkable thing.

What has led to a situation that a population of a country is begging the authorities to be allowed to introduce more draconian measures that restrict them like never before?

FEAR.

Fear is such a powerful motivator, coupled with a powerful media, every minute of every day of rolling coverage – to the exclusion of all other news – even the usual 'funny' story at the end of the news that cheers us all up has made a sharp withdrawal – I'm sure deemed as being too insensitive at this time.

Pictures of dead bodies in bags, usually restricted from mainstream television to protect the audience, were shown in the early stages to make everyone aware of how serious the virus was.

This virus is being painted as so virulent and so dangerous that the media are taking no chances. This needs to be resolved globally so the whole world can go back to 'a new reality' – whatever this is deemed to be.

The virus is telling a truly powerful story and we are getting the sense it will change our lives forever going forward.

In addition to the many challenges, many good things are happening during the lockdown. New relationships are being created in the virtual world and families and friends who previously rarely had time for each other are coming together and spending 'virtual' time together.

The apps like Zoom which bring people together have seen their value go up manyfold in a matter of weeks as the whole way we run our life has metamorphosed in an instant – and the need for connection, however it can be achieved, is vital for our survival.

One fascinating thing has happened to all of us since Covid started and that is a flight to where we feel safest and a flight to our truth.

I have noticed that we have attached ourselves even closer to the people in our lives that we truly value and we have distanced ourselves from people who we value less, for whatever reason.

We have also reconnected with many of our old friends with whom we were close in our past.

This is a totally subconscious happening playing out in our conscious world. Something we have no control of at all - even if we think we have.

In extreme circumstances, which these are, our survival mechanism kicks in and guides us and leads us to the people and things we truly need and are the 'truth' in our life.

The big question is post virus, what will happen to our lovely world? There are currently very few planes in the sky, less car journeys being taken, we are getting used to a new normal and many of us are enjoying it spending more time at home being with our family and working at the same time.

You can already hear the conversations in the boardrooms around the world speculating about what the 'new world' will look and feel like.

Having worked from home for over a year, a 'proof of concept' will have taken place and will have proved to have been successful in so many companies and saved a huge fortune in allocated costs.

With the clamour about 'Climate Change' ringing loud in the ears of a world that cries out for more safety and connection, getting louder and louder every day, one can imagine that things will not go back to the same way they were before.

There will be an enormous pressure, I'm sure, backed by the main G7 countries and governments in the world to make some or many of these changes permanent – which will be to the benefit of so many in all areas of society.

The planet surely must learn the most important lesson of all from this wake-up call – just in time to save the planet, from what many see, as its ultimate destruction.

The pollution on the planet has reduced remarkably and there are many winners from this situation. We have all seen pictures from space of the 'before and after Covid' pictures of major cities with significantly less pollution.

I have also seen a study that 'seismic activity' has reduced markedly since the global lockdown started which is another indicator that man is partly responsible for the many earthquakes, tsunamis and volcanoes that have been happening recently.

Inspirational thought to leave you with.

You can judge me afterwards as I sit here today and I'm sensing that the powerful Climate Change lobby, together with many of the major countries in the world will ensure that a new normal is created, that will still allow the same level of wealth creation yet lead to a future that will allow the planet to not just survive but to thrive.

I am sensing that a 'new reality' is already happening in our minds which will change the direction of the planet forever. Let us wait and see how this plays out shall we? I am sure I will be writing more about this in my next book.

Chapter 21
Final Thoughts

Wow! That was a journey of uncovering our deeper wisdom and truths indeed and thank you so much for joining me in this magic of self-discovery and learning.

It is a truly beautiful thing that you can take simple ideas and concepts and bring them into your everyday lives today and truly make a difference to your mindsets, attitudes and beliefs.

We have experienced so many magical ideas, principles, adventures, thoughts and feelings and I sense we have gone on a remarkable journey of discovery together.

We have journeyed from being calm and content in our 'Happy Place' to understanding better the power of music and animals in our lives. We have been on trains, climbed mountains and told beautiful stories. We have embarked on a journey of discovery that will last a lifetime and will only become deeper and more powerful as we all grow and develop and learn.

As I mentioned in the Introduction, finding your panacea is connecting you to the source of life itself and what connects us all at a deeper level to each other and the universe by an invisible thread of collective consciousness.

You will only reach your own panacea if you complete the first step which is more deeply knowing yourself, loving yourself, understanding yourself and connecting with your inner truth and wisdom and in effect, your essence. It is creating the belief within you that you deserve all the things that happen to you and you are worthy of all of them.

Having read the book, you will now be a small step closer to reaching your own panacea of understanding within you and you are at the start of your voyage of personal discovery.

Always keep reading and learning and expanding your wisdom and let us create a community together where we can share ideas, thoughts and feelings about our lives.

I am in the process of writing the second book and am happy to incorporate any ideas that you have for the content.

I would very much love this to be an interactive journey for all of us and I have created a pages on Social Media called the **Panacea Principles** and I would really value any feedback, thoughts and ideas for the future.

Keeping believing, keep learning and keep BEING true to yourself and you will find the panacea that you seek.

Allen Martin - Biography

The Panacea Principles is Allen's first book as an author and a wonderful opportunity for him to put all of his many learnings from life, career, psychology and classroom and coaching sessions into one place – and to help everyone reading this book to become even better versions of themselves.

Allen Martin is an Executive Coach, Author and People Development trainer, helping people to become even better versions of themselves and become even more aware of their personal strengths and areas of development.

Allen is passionate about helping people to discover the wisdom and self confidence within themselves and his 'people-centric' approach has a powerful impact on individuals enabling them to discover and reach their full potential.

Allen has delivered hundreds of classroom training sessions globally and over 200 hours of face to face 1-1 coaching sessions. Allen's classroom sessions are totally interactive and fun, whilst at the same time imparting deep mindset shifting learning that resonates fundamentally with all who attend the classses.

Allen creates interactive and powerful content daily on social media and hosts the One Minute of Wisdom Video series (#One1MinuteOfWisdom) and a @DailyMindsetShifters page on Facebook.

Career

After starting out in retail banking in his early career with NatWest Bank, Allen spent over 30 years in Investment Banking, working initially with SG Warburg before spending 24 years at HSBC Investment Bank.

At HSBC Allen held several management positions in Treasury areas including Futures and Options and the last 9 years in Learning and Development as a People Development Trainer and Coach.

As well as working in the Financial Services Industry, Allen has more recently developed his skill-set as a consultant into the retail commodities industry, travel media sectors and specifically on-line zoom training, writing and coaching.

Professional Qualifications

- Academy of Executive Coaching (AOEC) Practitioner
- Neuro Linguistic Programming (NLP) Practitioner
- Institute of Linguists - Italian (Preliminary/ Intermediate and Advanced)
- ITIM - Lecturer – Organisational Culture and Change

Acknowledgements

This book is dedicated to many influential people in my life who have guided me and helped me become the person that I am today. They say you can count the people of true value on one hand and those of you who are close to me know who you are.

This - my first book – is dedicated to all of you and THANK YOU from the bottom of my heart for helping me and supporting me throughout my life.

Some of you have been there my whole life and some of you have come into my life recently – you are all beautiful humans and I value you all greatly.

Printed in Great Britain
by Amazon